A STARTER
KIT TO
JOY

CHRISTA L. SMITH

**Manufactured in the United
States of America**

ISBN: 979-8-9883985-0-9

Library of Congress
Control Number: 2023909469

Follow Christa Smith

Instagram @igniteyourlife.co
Email: info@igniteyourlifeco.com
Website: www.igniteyourlifeco.com

CONTENTS

Foreword. 1

The Spark 3

Journey To Joy-Exploration 15

Step 1 - Be Still 25

Step 2 - Affirm 33

Step 3 - Move 41

Step 4 - Practice/Reflect. 49

Step 5 - Rejoice/Celebrate You!. . 57

Exhale. 63

Recap - A Starter Kit To Joy . . . 65

Resources 67

Acknowledgement 69

Biography 73

This book is dedicated to my Dad.
Once there was a silly ol' ant...

Foreword

I will never forget the day I first met Christa Smith over twenty years ago. She walked into my office and instantly grabbed my attention with her air of confidence, intelligence, and beauty. Being a woman who usually played it safe, I felt a connection to her immediately; wanting to be around this person who had such immense power within her. Since then, she's helped me realize my true potential as an individual, getting closer to understanding who I am and what truly makes me happy. Christa has been the catalyst for my transformation into the best version of myself over the years, something I could have never imagined, inspiring me towards success as a best-selling author and a thriving entrepreneur. Her natural ability to uplift and show you how capable you are is remarkable; she's raw, real, incredibly strong, and electrifyingly loving in one powerful package!

If you ever felt like life was missing something, but you weren't quite sure what would give it that spark, with "A Starter Kit to Joy", Christa provides a unique look into discovering the beauty of life through inner transformation. By embracing her guidance and giving yourself a chance to explore yourself from within, you will uncover unexpected gemstones waiting for you. Whether it's uncovering self-love or gaining clarity in your purpose and goals, you get to experience and embrace a beautiful life that you never could have even imagined! The journey with Christa is motivating, inspiring and truly an enriching one, so why not take that leap? You won't regret it.

Nikki Boyd
At Home with Nikki
Best-selling Author of "Beautifully Organized, A guide to function and style in your home"

The Spark

My life changed when my father died. You truly never know how death will change you until it happens. He had already been in the hospital for a few months so there had been some 'prep' time. Being a realist, I had utilized that time to take inventory of how I would feel without him, recognizing that it was best for him to pass through this lifetime, and I prepared myself accordingly. And then he died. I was devastated. The finality of death is just that, final. No more - as if a part of you has been cut off. Forever.

I am a single mother and have been for a long time. The struggle is REAL! Or it had been. At that particular time in my journey, I had just built my first house after divorce. During the building process, I had moved in with my dad and stepmom. Little did I know what a blessing that would be for me. I spent five months with my dad before his passing. Looking back, even though that time could be described as aggravating, suffocating and crazy, I also recognize that it was priceless. I am so thankful to the Universe for getting in the way of me buying a house that would have been ready sooner. I was going to put an offer on a house that was already started but someone else got to it a day before me. A single day. At the time, I had been upset because that meant staying longer in my parents' house. But, as usual, the things that cause us frustration and pain, are often the source of our most poignant blessings.

After my father's death, I, the Queen of Damn Near Everything, went into a deep depression. I was able to find the energy to go to work and produce because, frankly, I had no choice. But being able to care for my children was a distant second. Caring for myself wasn't even a thought. I was grateful for prepped meal deliveries like Home

Chef and others; they helped me put food on the table without too much thought or effort. If DoorDash had been available back then I would be in the poor house!

My grief was so strong that I wanted to wear black for a year, like in Victorian times, so people would know what was wrong with me; they would understand why I wasn't functioning on all cylinders.

I knew I needed to do something different. I needed to figure out how to pull myself out of this rut.

You see, my father had been a ruminator. During one of our last conversations, alone in his living room, he asked me about our time in St. Thomas and if I ever thought back to that time. I asked "Why would I? It's in the past." I wasn't one to dwell on things. I felt like that's how people stayed stuck, and I was all about moving forward. Through a series of events, I finally received the message. My best friend from St. Thomas, helped me understand that you can't get *over* anything until you move *through* it. So, my method of leaving everything in the past wasn't the healthiest method for forward movement.

I ruminated on this. ☺

I had learned throughout my childhood, from the adults in my life, that emotions were messy and often got in the way of getting things done.

Tasks needed to be completed, so my siblings and I did what was necessary. I grew up in a family of divorce and learned to keep people and situations in boxes. Dad's family life went in this box. Mom's went into another. School friends stayed in their own box not to mix with neighborhood friends and so on. I compartmentalized everything. As a result, I never found a safe place to express my whole self since there were no areas of my boxed-up life that would allow for it. I kept my feelings inside and moved them to a place I imagined as a trash can and promptly disposed of them. Recently, I realized that all those feelings have just been stuffed down and compacted. I had not moved through them. Until recently, I was not ready to process them.

You see, timing truly is everything. Your connection with this book isn't a mistake. It is the right time for you. It doesn't matter if you treat it as your personal bible to help you move towards JOY and purpose, or you read just a bit of it. It all comes down to exposure and the divine right timing for your journey.

Life is not about perfection, it is an experiment. You can't get it wrong. There may be room for improvement, but you can't get it wrong. When you make a 'mistake', you'll see that it turns into a lesson that you needed to move through. These lessons will keep showing up to give you practice until you master them. You will then be able to move on to the next lesson life has in store for you.

Okay, so back to my journey. I was sitting in my brand-new living room with a gorgeous view of the surrounding trees and I desperately wanted to be happy, or to get out of my funk, my stuck-in-the-mud-ness. So, after my 'year' of grieving and wearing black, what did I decide to tackle but weight loss? I started using the Noom app and it changed my life. Now, full disclosure, I didn't lose much weight, but it got me thinking about why I was eating the way I did. *Where did this need to fill a void come from and how could I use other things, besides food, to feel fulfilled?*

Noom has daily questions that it asks you and one of these questions asked what brought me JOY. I was so happy to list the things that brought me JOY that even the process of doing so brought me JOY. It put me in the energy of that JOY just by thinking of those things.

At the same time, my friend gifted me with a daily calendar, The Secret, by Rhonda Byrne. I liked that the inspirational sayings weren't linked to an actual day of the month. The calendar was set up for motivational sayings for each day of the week but not a specific time in the month. So I never felt behind if I missed a day, or several. I was able to pick it up at anytime, choosing the day of the week and the daily message. On one particular day, when I was so keen to document all the things that brought me JOY, the calendar asked me to write down 100 things I was grateful for. That task seemed so huge, I put the calendar down for at least a month. 100 things! An impossible task! Shortly after that, I went to visit my sister in NY. I was sharing this story with her and she said, "I am not sure I could write down what brings me JOY, but it would be easy to write 100 things I am grateful for." That stopped me in my tracks.

Then I started thinking, *Is there that much difference between what you are grateful for and things that bring you JOY?* It makes sense that you would be grateful for all of the things that bring you JOY, although maybe not all things you are grateful for reach a level of actual JOY. Still similar, nonetheless. This was the block that I needed to be reframed so I could see a path forward.

Several months went by and I was learning more and more about manifesting and co-creating my reality with God/Source/Universe; intentional living. Even if it is all hokey pokey, which it can often sound like it at first, I had rediscovered the feeling of excitement and well-being. I began taking time to visualize what I wanted. I began to truly expand my thoughts, going beyond the drudgery of my current life.

This took root in me and spread like wildfire. I was totally into this manifesting thing. Sure, I got discouraged in the beginning when I wanted something, put forth my efforts in visualizing and aligning myself up with my desire and then it didn't happen. However, I have since learned that my ego was getting in the way; I needed to learn how to trust more. I needed to trust that the Universe/God has my back and always sees the bigger picture. I am a co-creator after all, not the sole creator.

The journey to JOY starts with trusting in forces outside of yourself; i.e.

God/Universe. There is magic in the way things unfold. When you think about it, your birth in and of itself was a miracle. How magical it was for that sperm and that egg to meet at that exact time to create you! I grew up Catholic, but I am not traditionally religious. Rather, I am deeply spiritual and believe in Divine Right Timing and co-creation with a life source that is greater than me. Some call this God and others, Universe. I interchange them and see them as the same greater life force.

What truly moved me to write this book, was the epiphany that by incorporating a few basic steps into my life, my world was changed drastically for the better. I was living my best life at the same time as our world came down with a pandemic and social injustice was visually plaguing our country again. I am, in no way, minimizing the impact of the pandemic and all the lives that were lost (and that we are still losing). While all this was going on around me, and worldwide fear was prevalent,

I kept my focus on the things that were working well, the gifts that the Universe was giving me.

I recognized the expansion of self that working from home gave me. I was able to have the connection, via Zoom, with family and friends that had been missing before. I was given space to examine my life and take stock of who I was internally. The silence of the outside world allowed me to dig deep into what brought me JOY and to my life's purpose. What am I passionate about? What do I want out of life without considering limitations?

I saw so many of my friends and community members suffering, and I wanted to help them to look at life the way that I was. I noticed that when I shared certain perspectives with family and friends they took to it.

I listened to different YouTube videos and meditations and started a daily journal practice along with a gratitude reflection at night before I went to bed; reflecting on what went well that day.

I was sure there had to be an easily accessible formula to provide to people that they could use as a model for living a JOY filled life. *What would that look like?*

As a result, A Starter Kit to JOY was created; five simple steps to keep you on track to being your authentic self. Five steps that will require major effort in order to create a new mindset. Once achieved, the five steps can keep you steady on the path like bumper guards on a bowling lane.

This book is a kick start for your unique journey. We all have various life lessons we need to work through. A journey to JOY takes dedication and practice just like anything else in life that you want to excel at. The more you practice, the easier it becomes; second nature even. It will soon stop feeling like work as a new pattern of positivity emerges and becomes your true internal map.

I hope it helps you as it has helped me: to live a more JOYous harmonious life! Cheers!

JOURNEY TO
JOY-EXPLORATION

The embodiment of JOY is a wonderful thing. It can also be scary; like navigating unknown territory. Connecting, or reconnecting, to our inner selves allows us to cultivate JOY. As we build that connection and begin to heal ourselves, we also heal the world with one loving gesture at a time.

How can you love yourself more?

By saying yes to you!

How is it you can do that, you ask?

Stop
Be still
Listen

What brings you JOY? Do you have a list that instantly pops up in your mind or is it easier to start with things that feel good? Or does your mind draw a blank when you think about JOY?

Often, we are conditioned, as women, to focus on the things that need to be done. The endless tasks that include excelling at work, being a mom, sister, daughter, significant other. With this constant cycle of *doing,* we've given up thinking about ourselves; our needs, hopes and dreams, much less what brings us JOY. If you ask us about anyone in our lives and what they like and what gets their engines running, I assure you we will have an answer. But when asking ourselves those same questions, we are often non-plussed, having always put others first. If we manage to come up with something, our list isn't extensive.

We generally fill our time with tasks, whether it be cleaning, working, being a chauffeur, going to practice, working out, or listening to music; we rarely take time to be still. Even when we don't over schedule ourselves, we have been so programmed to always *go* and always *do* that we don't know what to do with ourselves when there is silence. Generally, we will pick up a book or listen to YouTube or watch TikTok or scroll through Facebook. When we consistently fill the silence, we leave no room for hearing our intuition or what our bodies are really telling us.

As babies, we demanded what we needed: to be fed, nurtured and clothed/ diapers changed. However, along the way, as our screams and cries weren't answered, we had to adapt.

In the Fundamentals of Enneagram blog by Samantha Mackay, she comments that your personality develops as a way to manage the pain of not getting your needs met. "And what was once a health adaptation becomes a series of limiting beliefs, used to defend against and avoid revisiting the pain from your most vulnerable years."

What coping mechanisms served you well in the past but are no longer helping you thrive?

What behavior patterns do you notice about yourself?

How were they influenced?

Can you name what stands in the way between you and JOY other than your parents, boss, significant other or children?

The timeline of moving towards JOY is different for each of us. It can depend on what inner demons and narratives we have playing in a loop in our minds. True JOY requires us to move through the things we fear and have faith that we can conquer them in this lifetime. As Joseph Campbell said, "The cave you fear to enter holds the treasure you seek. Fear of the unknown is our greatest fear. Many of us would enter a dark cave. While caution is a useful instinct, we lose many opportunities and much of the adventure of life if we fail to support the curious explorer within us. We must let go of the life we have planned, so as to accept the one that is waiting for us."

Brené Brown says, "You either walk inside your story and own it or you stand outside your story and hustle for your worthiness."

How have you been hustling?

Finding your JOY is a simple task. If you can identify what drives you nuts, you can see the beauty in the flip side, the opposite. Ask yourself some questions about the actions or events in your life that you don't appreciate.

What patterns occur over and over for you?

How would your life look if these roadblocks dissipated?

When you can identify what you don't like, you can then reflect on what you do want.

What bubbles up for you?

By focusing on what you do want, things begin to appear, floating to the surface of your consciousness, things that you truly enJOY or want to try. These bubbles of ideas will eventually lead to greater understanding of what sparks your passions and ultimately your JOY.

Part of listening and giving voice to what brings you JOY is honoring your feminine energies. Owning your responsibilities is more of a masculine energy. Masculine energy is needed, but over the decades of our do-do-do mode, an imbalance of masculine energy has developed. It is time for all of us to honor the feminine energy that is within. When honoring this energy, it allows us to connect with self, which in turn facilitates deeper connections with others. It is healing and nurturing. It enables us to allow things to occur, versus doing everything ourselves.

During our quest for JOY, our job is to listen to ourselves and learn more about ourselves by doing so. Once we understand ourselves and our true motivations, passions, and purpose, we can go beyond that and be present for others.

When we fuel ourselves, we facilitate the sharing of that healing energy with others. Joseph Campbell emphasized this sentiment with this quote, "We're not on our journey to save the world but to save ourselves. But in doing that you save the world. The influence of a vital person vitalizes." And each of us is vital.

A rebalancing of masculine and feminine energies is needed in order to create better harmony in our lives and henceforth, the world.

How can we support ourselves and then others?

How do we get to know our most authentic selves?

First, quiet the noise, listen within.

Breathe.

Breathe again.

What do you like about yourself?

Emphasize it.

It's true what they say, thoughts become things. If you are struggling to identify what you do like about yourself, think about the traits that you would like to emphasize within your daily life. Choose what you want to embody.

It is ok to fear your own thoughts. It is important to give them a voice and then release the thoughts into the Universe so that you are no longer holding on tight to them. Releasing those self- limiting beliefs helps you move through the fear.

One exercise that you can do, as suggested by Gabby Bernstein, is to give yourself 5 minutes and "Rage on the Page". Write down all the things that scare you, that make you mad, that irritate you; get it out of your system. In a symbolic gesture, you can burn the page(safely) and let the earth take those scary thoughts away, transforming them into positive energy.

Do you ever wonder who you are at your core?

What inspires you?

What are YOU passionate about?

What gifts come to you effortlessly?

What are you meant to do/be?

What is your life's purpose?

These questions may seem heavy, but they don't have to be. It is important for us to be honest with ourselves as we ask and answer these questions. We don't need to feel like we need to save the world or make a huge impact outside of our circle or community. Some people have expressed that their purpose is to provide for their family and to live a better life than they had growing up. Others are great story tellers and know they are meant to write books or publish their work. What do you feel your calling is? It has been said that you are an expert when you have spent over 10,000 hours doing something. What's the something you are an expert in?

Throughout history, women have given up our power, as demonstrated by our (white) male dominated world. How do we reclaim it?

We are powerful! Our feminine energy is strong, soft and alluring. We are commanding, fluid and nurturing. Feminine energy is awesome! We reclaim it by starting with ourselves. I have identified 5 steps that helped me with coming into harmony with myself and have allowed me to live more JOYously that I think can help you too.

Are you ready to move up the mountain of JOY and celebrate each step along the way??

Come with me. Let's get it. Let's GO!!

STEP 1 - BE STILL

There are three components to Step 1, the first of which is to be still. Schedule YOU time to allow yourself to meditate/be in the quiet and journal.

Give yourself at least 5 minutes in the morning before you give yourself to others and your day. I found that 10 minutes for meditation and 10 minutes for journaling was the best amount of time for me. If you feel that you don't have 10 minutes, start with 5 minutes each.

Tell everyone, especially yourself, that you deserve this uninterrupted time. As you get more comfortable with allotting time for yourself, start to increase it.

Once you have carved out time for yourself, use it to center/ground yourself for the day. If you don't want to practice guided meditations, simply set a gentle timer and do some deep breathing. This can easily be done while you wait for your coffee or tea to brew. If coffee and tea aren't your thing, just take a moment to sit with your eyes closed and breathe. Breathe in for a count of 4 and out for a count of 6; repeat this 10 times.

Focus on your breath. Allow thoughts to flow in and out. I recommend a guided meditation that is of an empowering nature. You can find both religious and non-religious meditations on YouTube or other streaming platforms.

Guided meditations take the pressure off those interfering thoughts and also give voice to those good-feeling thoughts that can naturally help set intentions for the day.

Be kind to yourself. You can't get it wrong. If your inner voice starts to criticize and potentially berate you, just tell it that you can't get it wrong and to leave you alone (for 5 to 10 minutes). ☺ Do the same if you find yourself making a list for later… let that inner voice know that it isn't time for that right now.

In the beginning, when several messages about meditation crossed my path, I poo-pooed them. It seemed too weird honestly. Just shut off your thoughts and breathe in silence. What? How can you shut off your thoughts? But I am studious, so I tried it. It was around this time that I purchased a vibrating machine - no not a vibrator ☺; a platform designed for moving and shaking your body to get the blood circulating. Its cycle lasted for 10 minutes. I decided to balance myself on it, close my eyes and hum. "Ohmmmmmmmmmm" "Ohmmmmmmmmmmm"

A thought would float in, and I would refresh my Ohms and the thought would float away. I got used to doing this for 10 minutes while on my vibration machine. I was an amusing sight for my children when they woke up and saw me humming and vibrating but, hey, I was trying to get out of my funk.

I have never been a big researcher online, so it must have been one of my friends that sent me one of my first guided meditations. When I first listened to it, it was like the heavens opened and the angels were singing. I was stunned – *You mean I didn't have to do this all on my own? I could feel good by just plugging in, following along, and letting go.* I thought I must be cheating; it was so easy. I got really good at manifesting the right meditation for myself each morning. I tried all kinds, including Deepak Chopra with Alicia Keys 21-Day Meditation Experience: The Divine Feminine, but my favorite YouTube channel for meditation is *Great Meditation*. I had to figure out that it was okay that I didn't like all meditations. It was a good lesson for me to allow myself not to listen until the end if I wasn't resonating with the meditation guide. Some people prefer a man's voice, others prefer a woman's. Some sound more computer generated than others, some sound quality is better than others and so on. Part of my journey was finding those that I liked and being okay with the fact that I didn't like all of them.

During your dedicated time in the morning after (or before) mediation/ silence, start a daily journal practice. At first, you can just sit down and write what comes to mind, even if that's "I don't know what comes to mind and this feels weird." ☺ Give yourself five minutes to journal each day. The more consistent you are with giving yourself that time, the more likely it will become a habit.

As you get into the habit of journaling, write down anything that brings you JOY. It can be anything from watching butterflies in a field to playing games in an arcade. It could even be your bucket list of things you want to experience in life. Be sure to give yourself grace as your journaling process evolves. Some may take to writing and need more than five minutes a day. Others may feel stagnant.

It is important to hold the time and space for journaling and listen to whatever is coming up for you.

As you start to identify your JOYous things, also begin to ensure you carve time out for yourself to 'do' them.

Newton's third law states that "If an object A exerts force on object B, then object B must exert a force of equal magnitude and opposite direction back on object A". One application of Newton's third law is that the more JOYous things you start doing the more JOY comes back to you.

By journaling and allowing yourself to identify what kinds of things you like, you will be able to use this journaling time to incorporate some of these things into your schedule. Set your intentions for the day. How would you like the day to turn out? What would you like to accomplish with ease?

When I first started my journey to JOY, I had to develop a routine for writing in my journal. I thought, *Why bother; I am already sharing the thoughts with myself in my head*? *Why write them down?* Then I started to journal and I discovered that the release it gave me was incredibly helpful; I no longer had to hold onto the thoughts. At first, my journaling was similar to a to-do list, it soon evolved to allow me to also reflect on what I wanted out of my day. It provided me with time and space that was mine and mine alone. It felt like a best friend who wasn't bothered by all my thoughts and problems. Ideas began to blossom as I re-read what I wrote. When I was formulating what I wanted to write, other thoughts that were more productive would seep in. Now I don't go anywhere without a journal with some blank pages because I never know when I will want to capture what I am feeling on paper.

RECAP- Step 1- Be Still

❖ Schedule YOU time in the morning

❖ Meditate

❖ Journal Daily

STEP 2 - AFFIRM

After Step One, where you've taken the time to ground yourself for the day and set your intentions during your journaling time, now it is time to continue the process. Be sure to daydream. Dream big; contemplate what you want out of the day or life in general. Do this without limitations. Next, start an active practice of gratitude. Use affirmations to shift your current beliefs to a better reality. The more you say things the more you begin to believe them. The more you believe, the more you manifest. The more you manifest, the easier it is to believe, and the momentum propels you forward to what you once thought was impossible.

Start training your inner voice (the one that is more critical than your worst enemy or your mother) to give you grace because you deserve it. Would you allow this inner voice to say the same things to your best friend? Stop allowing it to talk to you in a negative way. It is time to start giving more power to the goodness that is you. Release the self-limiting thoughts.

Start where you are. Identify where you want to be.

If you had a magic wand, how would your day look?

Would it be filled with struggle and challenges that feel insurmountable?

I think not.

A simple intention could be: *It would be great if my day was filled with ease.* Then sit with the feeling of that ease. Let it build up all around you. What would need to go right in order for that to happen?

Try not to limit yourself to logic. Logic is likely how you got to this not-so-great feeling. Focus on all the ways life will be easy. Just sit with the thought, in this case one of ease, and truly let that feeling wash over you. What does that feel like?

I used to think daydreaming was just a time where you would get your hopes up only to come crashing back to reality or disappointment. So why dream about that big, humongous beach house, or that perfect life partner? I was a realist. What were the odds of that happening? What would have to happen for those things to become a reality? I soon realized those thoughts were self-limiting. Why should I get in the way of what could happen?

Mike Dooley, from The Universe Talks, shared an exercise of how to manifest your goals. Start by drawing a triangle with a goal written at the top. On one side of the triangle write down all the things that are needed to reach the goal. On the other side, write down all the unknowns in accomplishing your goal. These are the things that the Universe/ God needs to do in order for the goal to be reached. Completing this exercise allowed me to see which actions I could take myself and those that felt unsurmountable that I needed the Universe/God to assist with. Co-creating is putting your wishes, wants and desires out into existence and then freeing yourself from controlling the outcome of how it happens. Releasing control over all possible outcomes is freeing once you are able to truly succumb. It is nerve-wracking at first to give up control to unseen forces and frankly anything outside of yourself. You have been successful in life so far because of planning for the worst-case scenario. How can you give up that control? 'Planning' for the best case relies on a greater force than yourself to see it to fruition. This isn't an easy process, but it can, and will, be reinforced the more you give credence to it. Once something gains momentum the more and more those daydreams become reality!

Incorporating gratitude in your daily practice is also essential. It helps with the positivity momentum and results in the manifestation of feel-good outcomes. One way to do this is to become more aware and present throughout the events of the day and evaluate them in comparison to your expectations.

What ended up being easy? Celebrate those moments! Become your own cheerleader.

If, upon self-reflection, you can't think of anything that was easy for you that day - think about how you didn't have to put any effort into continuously breathing. Ease can also show up in the way we wash our hands with the running water that is at our disposal. Or even appreciating how the birds sing in the morning and flowers bloom.

Momentum is a powerful tool. Use it to your advantage. The more gratitude you express, the more things show up for you to be grateful for.

As you gain momentum in recognizing the things you want, journal about them and even dare to dream bigger. If you had a magic wand, how would you wave it? What would you ask for? What dreams do you want to become a reality? Give yourself permission to dream big!

What do you want?

Think in terms of desire, not just about what is or how circumstances will or can get in the way of your desire. Just sit with what it is that you want. Start a side hustle of being a daydreamer!

Everyone needs genuine recognition and appreciation. Everyone wants to be seen. I started talking to my plants in the morning on the way to my meditation spot. "Thank you for thriving", I said. I was never a green thumb and having manifested these plants, I wanted to do right by them. So, I thanked them every day and night and they are indeed thriving. The plants are flourishing so brilliantly, people now ask me for plant advice.

I also thank the Universe for helping me with certain things throughout the day - no line at my favorite drive-through that's always packed or getting through all my emails during the workday or having ease with what could've been a difficult conversation with my daughter.

I found once I started, I was able to keep going with the appreciation and more and more things surfaced to appreciate.

Some days can be frustrating, and it takes more effort than others to actually see the positive. Maybe something 'blows up' and the first emotion isn't one of gratitude, but eventually the benefit of the 'blow up' is revealed. I am then able to file it away to offer perspective for the next time there is a 'blow up'.

When you regularly practice gratitude for the things that are going well, you will get to a point where things are totally working out for you often. Affirm what you want into existence. You will be amazed at all the great things that show up for you!

RECAP- STEP 2- AFFIRM

- ❖ Set Daily Intentions

- ❖ Dream BIG

- ❖ Express Gratitude for big and small things

STEP 3 - MOVE

I'm not suggesting you move your residence although if that works for you, go for it! I'm talking about moving your body. Try different outings or take new classes. Be sure to connect with others and get outside your comfort zone.

Energy can't survive without movement. It is important to move your body, almost as important as it is to move your thoughts.

I was recently introduced to Authentic Sound Healing. It starts with a long, exaggerated sigh. Doing this relieves the tension held inside your body. One exercise I resonated with was asking a body part what sound it made and then letting that sound come out of my mouth. I was surprised how cathartic it was. It also allowed me to understand my aches and pains more. Some other ways you can consider moving are as follows:

- ❖ Walk- inside or outside
- ❖ Dance like no one is watching!
- ❖ Run
- ❖ Bike ride
- ❖ Yoga
- ❖ Pilates
- ❖ Chair dance
- ❖ Sing/Sigh

Movement and sound are free and are only limited by your choices.

Movement was a hard one for me. Life had gotten me so exhausted. Being a career woman and single mother, I was too tired to make time to move. I knew logically this wasn't healthy (but didn't know how to realize positive change). Then something crossed my path; I realized that by starting the practice of movement it could also change the momentum of all things. So, I did what I could. I found an app called BodyGroove that contained five-minute dance segments for all sizes and abilities and that got me moving. It was motivating because the timeframe was doable for me. It allowed me to complete a challenge as well as search for a specific type of dance in the app. I literally danced like no one was watching and it brought out more of my feminine energy. I felt graceful even if I might not have looked the part! It was encouraging. It became the impetus for me to start wearing dresses, due to the flow of the movement of dance. Wearing a dress gave me the same easy-flowing feeling.

Weight, for me, has always been a challenge. I wasn't always overweight, but I was usually bigger than just about anyone in my circle. Even in high school I was bigger than all the football players except one. Although, looking back at photos, I was not very big at all.

Weight also can be a deterrent to connecting with others and going to new groups or classes. It was something I had to overcome little by little and in some ways still do. I can honestly say that I now feel more comfortable in my body than I ever have felt before in my life. I am also the heaviest I have ever been. I have moved through the guilt and shame of 'knowing better' about my food choices. By being able to move through these feelings, rather than pushing them down, I now look to eat healthily when I can. I am a work in progress and so is my relationship with food. I am accepting of that. I appreciate every ounce of my body no matter the way it presents itself to the world or how it may ache or not ache on any specific day. I have many more wonderful days of movement than I do of not moving, and I rejoice in that! My body has gotten me through so much in life, I couldn't live without it!

Part of finding JOY is connecting with others. As a self-identified introvert, doing things in the community is a challenge for me. I identified the things that were important and I found the inner strength, through affirmations and meditations, to put my foot out there. More often than not I was rewarded for my efforts and even when my efforts felt like epic fails, I learned more about what I wanted to experience going forward.

Recently, I took an art class in acrylic painting. At first, I was embarrassed; I had to ask what the difference between acrylic and oil paint was. I thought they were the same thing and brought oil paints to the class! I reminded myself that it was okay that I didn't know, and it was okay to not do something as 'it should be'. I also learned in that class that free-form painting was uncomfortable for me due to the feeling of true vulnerability of putting paint to paper. Sometimes the image represented what was in my head but often it did not! But it was a conversation piece. I was always amazed at the feedback, things that my fellow classmates saw that I didn't see, in my own painting. It was a good life lesson: when you allow yourself to be vulnerable you can learn even more about yourself through the eyes of others.

It is important to find support that feels good for you. If you are able to get a family member or friend to join this journey to JOY with you – wonderful! If you are not, no worries. Technology allows us to connect in ways we never have before. You don't have to do it all yourself. There are groups you can meet up with in person or join virtually. There are influential videos and other streaming pathways filled with encouragement and consciousness of living; manifesting the life you deserve. Podcasts or audio books are also a resource. And don't forget the library – it's free!

You are not alone on your Journey to JOY.

CHRISTA L. SMITH

RECAP- STEP 3- MOVE

- ❖ ~~Put your house on the market~~ Just kidding!

- ❖ Incorporate movement into your life daily.

- ❖ Try one new way to move:

  - ❖ Walking

  - ❖ Singing

  - ❖ Authentic sound-making

  - ❖ Dancing

- ❖ Ask someone to join you.

- ❖ Start a new routine that benefits you.

47

STEP 4 -
PRACTICE/REFLECT

Okay, so now you have started a daily/regular practice of making time for yourself, by meditating and journaling. You are taking time to affirm what you want and giving gratitude to your surroundings. Then, inevitably something will flare up that feels like it came out of the blue because, through your gratitude practice, you've reached a point where most days you are walking on air, or at least feeling good most of the time throughout the day. What do we do when something just pushes us from 0 to 100? Know and trust that this journey to JOY is just that - a journey. There will be times when your emotions will get the better of you.

When you get irritated, it will be more noticeable than it was before because you have already started training yourself to look for the positives based on the intentions you've set for the day.

Give voice to whatever it is that is irritating you. Do not stuff it down or away.

Get mad. Call or text a friend, and when you express what is bothering you, try to look at it from a view above, more objectively. "Rage on the Page" or yell and scream (in your car/home) or even find a safe place to break things (depending on the severity of the anger). Get it out of your system and then review. What was the cause and/or effect of the event? What occurred prior to it? Was it an event or a particular person that just aggravates the dickens out of you?

Above all, acknowledge your feelings and then release them. After getting the rage or frustration out of your system, thank your feelings for serving their purpose but also let them know you no longer need them to be so intense.

Now is the time to start retraining those thoughts. It is important to allow them to rise up, but it is equally as important to let them float by instead of allowing them to stay put and focusing on them.

After, or even during, the incident, but at a point where you can breathe deeply, it is time to reflect and to put into practice the work you have been doing. What did this aggravation highlight? What desire arose from this situation? What outcome would be one that is desirable? When something doesn't go 'right', consider what it is you would have wanted to have happened.

Out of contrast, comes clarity. Once you know what you really want to occur, you can shoot your rockets of desire and visualize. Sit with that dreamy intention.

How does that work? First, start with mind/body check-ins throughout the day. By doing so we are activating ourselves to be more conscientious of what is going on around us and within us. *How does my body feel? Is there tension or pain anywhere specific that shows up day after day? Is my stomach nervous from being in meetings all day? Do I have a sense of unease that's stemming from feeling incompetent or less than in a particular situation?* By doing these mind-body check-ins, you can start to gauge how your body reacts in these situations. By recognizing that, you can then begin to prepare somewhat for other situations that mirror these events and create healthy coping skills. The first step is identifying the physical and emotional reactions that arise.

When you notice that something does not feel good, give pause. Be still. Ask yourself: *What would feel better in this situation? What could I have done to choose the path that would feel good?*

Put that ideal outcome in your back pocket, ready to pull out at any time. As you encounter similar situations, bring up that memory and set your intention to what outcome you would ideally like to see happen.

Eckhart Tolle said, "All negativity is caused by an accumulation of psychological time and denial of the present. Unease, anxiety, tension, stress, worry- all forms of fear- are caused by too much future and not enough presence. Guilt, regret, resentment, grievances, sadness, bitterness, and all forms of non-forgiveness are caused by too much past, and not enough presence." In order to get to JOY, you must process your emotions and release those things that do not serve you. There are many ways to do this including, but not limited to, professional assistance.

The saying, practice makes perfect, is true. Now, I don't think any of us are truly looking for perfection, but practicing is hard work in the beginning. It becomes easier as you develop the skill. This applies to whatever you are working on. I remember, in the early days of my journey, even listening to motivational videos, while they were uplifting, they were also exhausting. My daily exhaustion shifted from having no energy because life beat me down to being exhausted from falling in love with my daydreams.

By putting the work into using these steps day in and day out, life became easier; life took less effort. It has gotten to the point where I often think of something and then it happens. *Did I pay that bill?* Oh look, a text reminder comes in that day to pay the bill I was thinking about. *Did I make that follow up appointment with the doctor?* I will need only to have that thought for the doctor's office to call me. Practice really does work. This is one area where making the effort is a worthwhile endeavor.

RECAP - STEP 4 - PRACTICE/REFLECT

- ❖ Give way to your emotions.

- ❖ Reframe Your experience.

- ❖ Identify what you do want from what you don't want- set intentions.

- ❖ Repeat

STEP 5-
REJOICE / CELEBRATE YOU!

Say YES to YOU

Ask yourself, what feels good to you?
Say yes to it. This is a big step to
get more in tune with yourself. It
can be one of the scariest steps.
*What will happen if I focus on saying
yes to me, to saying yes to what I
want? What actually feels good? Do I
even know?*

Women have been so focused on doing
for others, what happens when we turn
that energy onto ourselves?

We are natural givers. When we choose
to say yes to what feels good to us, it
has a ripple effect. Those we encounter
will feel the positive vibration of
our choices, as well. When we are
more content, it permeates to those
we encounter.

Giving yourself permission to remove the 'S' word (should) from your vocabulary is key to saying yes to yourself. When we are motivated to do something because we think we SHOULD, then we aren't usually honoring ourselves. We are acting out of obligation and therefore aren't enjoying what we are doing. Self-care and self-love is centered around reducing, or even eliminating, doing things because you should and focusing more on doing things you want to do or you will enjoy doing. When we decide to go down the path of agreeing to do something we feel we should be doing, it is essentially a self-sacrifice because our heart truly isn't in it. It, in essence, doesn't benefit us as a result. Self-care is self-love not self- sacrifice.

Saying yes to yourself often results in a big shake up for those you are close to. There is an adjustment period as we shift our priorities. Some family members and friends may not be too happy with the shift, with us saying no to them, as we say yes to ourselves. However, it will benefit everyone in the long run.

People are used to you being one way and changing your perspective to be more focused on yourself causes a shift. Typically, this means that people who have been relying on your support either emotionally or physically must now find new means by which to solve their problems. By saying no to others, you are actually giving them the opportunity to grow. Regardless of the gift you are giving them with a 'no', it doesn't usually feel good. Practice is essential. This is a big test of your own boundaries, and you are worth it! When you are able to fuel yourself, you also fuel others.

Now is the time to celebrate yourself. You are doing it! Taking steps to feel better is something to celebrate! Celebrate yourself along the way; no need to wait for a milestone. Give yourself an internal high-five or an external WHOOP WHOOP! Give yourself praise after journaling for several days in a row or seeing that what you set for your intentions in the morning really did show up for you that day.

Acknowledge your amazing self! You are exactly where you need to be on every step of the journey. Think about that. If you are exactly where you need to be, you can free yourself from having an expectation that you should be somewhere else on your journey.

You can't get it wrong.

If something doesn't go the way you want it to, it can help you create an even better outcome. You may also get the opportunity to keep facing the same challenges repeatedly until you have gained mastery and it makes sense for you to move in a different direction.

Celebrate YOU! Reward yourself and the accomplishment to choose good thoughts that feel good!

Treat yourself to something that enhances you and enhances your feminine power. You deserve it!

YOU ARE MAJESTIC!

"When you become comfortable with uncertainty, infinite possibilities open up in your life."
-Eckhart Tolle

RECAP - STEP 5- REJOICE/CELEBRATE YOU

- ❖ Start doing things that feel good to you.

- ❖ Say no to those things and people that don't.

- ❖ Give yourself grace-ALL the time.

- ❖ Give yourself verbal praise for your wins-big and small.

- ❖ Incorporate self-care into self-maintenance.

EXHALE

Even though these five steps are simple in nature, they can feel gargantuan as you move through them. These steps are an outline to help keep you on track towards your journey to JOY.

We have the power to write our own narrative. We can choose to look at things happening to us and focus on the injustice and drudgery of life, or we can flip our perspective so we are the stars in a story that looks for the positives to assist us in feeling good. When we are able to switch the narrative to one of appreciation and gratitude, we can truly become a student of life and learn and grow as designed.

You are worth your own time and dedication. Even if you are only able to give 10% to yourself of what you give to others, your life will improve. Living a more JOYous and harmonious life can be in your future, as well as your present, by living intentionally and using some of that intention towards yourself. These five steps are a guide to assist you on your journey.

Cheers to you and your success-whatever that looks like to you!

RECAP-A STARTER KIT TO JOY

- ❖ Schedule YOU time

- ❖ Meditate

- ❖ Journal

- ❖ Dream BIG

- ❖ Practice gratitude

- ❖ Set intentions daily

- ❖ Dance/Sing/Walk/Move

- ❖ Reframe your experiences

- ❖ Be kinder to yourself-update internal voice to one of a friend

- ❖ Recognize and celebrate what went right for you in your day and life

- ❖ EnJOY yourself-HAVE FUN

- ❖ Ask-What's the best thing that could happen?

- ❖ Give yourself GRACE

- ❖ Celebrate YOU!

- ❖ You can't get it wrong!!

Resources

YouTube Channels:

- ❖ Great Meditation-Any Meditation

- ❖ For Neal Yah-Love Yourself First by Louise Hay

- ❖ Lavendaire-Powerful Morning Affirmations

- ❖ Nick Keomahavong- 5 Things To Make Your Mornings Better

- ❖ Rising Higher Meditation-Go Within and Heal, Face Your Inner Self and DO THE WORK To Move Beyond The PAST and HEAL

- ❖ TEDx Talks- Happy Brain: How to Overcome Our Neural Predispositions to Suffering|Amit Sood,MD

Books:

- ❖ The Universe Has Your Back by Gabrielle Bernstein

- ❖ Finding Your Own North Star by Martha Beck

- ❖ The Untethered Soul by Michael A. Singer

- ❖ Gifts of Imperfection by Brené Brown

Acknowledgement

This book is dedicated to my family, starting with my dad. My life changed, for the better, after his passing. That sounds cruel but he has been able to help me tremendously through his passing and I know he is with me every day. While on earth my dad was an inspiration. He always made me feel important and valued; he was always interested in what I was thinking.

My parents were divorced, so I wasn't around him daily during my youth, but he did make the most of our time together. Often, we would ride bicycles back to my mother's house. I always enjoyed these rides. They allowed me to spend time out in nature and dedicated time with my dad. We would often sing songs and one song in particular was about ants: High

Hopes. The traditional lyrics were about a male ant, but my dad changed the pronouns to she/her. This song inspired me to do anything and be anything since this little ol' ant could move a rubber tree plant! A miracle! Thanks Dad!

My mother, as all mothers do, had a major impact on my growth and development. I was lucky that she celebrated life and instilled a sense of importance in me; from unique birthday cakes and gifts to buying a floor-length mirror where I could dance and dance and dance and develop confidence and a strong sense of self.

I also want to thank my stepmother for bringing a sense of levity to my upbringing that helped balance

things out when I was a teenager navigating between two homes.

To my sister in heaven, Chrissy, thank you so much for all the adventures you took me on! I forever thank you for getting me out of my comfort zones time and time again! Miss you.

To my older sister, thank you for showing me the way and how to get shit done! You are my rock! Your fortitude is AMAZING!

To my older brother, thank you for showing me how to have fun and enjoy the outdoors! Our time spent roughhousing during my youth is invaluable to me!

To my youngest sibling, you have opened my eyes to a new way of thinking and I am so glad you are in my life.

To my soul family, I truly couldn't have done this without you and your support sessions that ranged from making me laugh to cathartic cries. You are the bestests ever!!

To my beautiful daughters, you have truly opened my world so much I am thankful for your love and support as well as all the lessons you've enriched me with. You truly have helped my soul expand.

To my pup - my new ride-or-die bitch! We are going places!!

Biography

Christa L. Smith has always been passionate about helping others. She received her Bachelor's in Social Work in hopes of doing just that. For over 25 years she was an executive in healthcare revenue cycle where she split her time between helping patients get assistance for their hospital bills and collecting from insurance companies to ensure hospital doors stayed open.

During her healthcare career she also focused on growing leaders within her organizations by helping them work with their own strengths and getting to know themselves even more.

Recently she has branched off; focusing on helping women to identify their passions in order to live a more joyous and harmonious life. She is the founder and CEO of Ignite Your Life, LLC.

Christa lives in Midlothian, VA with her two adult daughters, on occasion, and her mini-Aussie doodle, Zola.

Journal Notes

_____

_____

_____

_____

_____

_____

_____

_____

_____

_____

_____

_____

_____

_____

_____

_____

_____

_____

_____

_____

_____

_____

_____

_____

_____

_____

_____

_____

_____

_____

_____

_____

_____

_____

_____

_____

_____

_____

_____

_____

_____

_____

_____

_____

_____

_____

_____

_____

_____

_____

_____

_____

_____

_____

_____

_____

_____

_____

_____

_____

_____

_____

_____

_____

_____

_____

_____

_____

_____

_____

_____

_____

_____

_____

_____

_____

_____

_____

_____

_____

_____

_____

_____

_____

_____

_____

_____

_____

_____

JOURNAL NOTES

JOURNAL NOTES

_____

_____

_____

_____

_____

_____

_____

_____

_____

_____

_____

_____

_____

_____

_____

_____

_____

_____

_____

_____

_____

_____

_____

_____

_____

_____

_____

_____

_____

_____

_____

_____

_____

_____

_____

_____

_____

_____

JOURNAL NOTES

124

Drawing

DRAWING

DRAWING

DRAWING

DRAWING

DRAWING

DRAWING

DRAWING

DRAWING

DRAWING

DRAWING

DRAWING

DRAWING

DRAWING

DRAWING

DRAWING

DRAWING

DRAWING

DRAWING

DRAWING

DRAWING

DRAWING

DRAWING

DRAWING

DRAWING

DRAWING

DRAWING

DRAWING

DRAWING

DRAWING

DRAWING

DRAWING

DRAWING

DRAWING

DRAWING

DRAWING

DRAWING

DRAWING

DRAWING

DRAWING

DRAWING

DRAWING

DRAWING

DRAWING

DRAWING

DRAWING

DRAWING

DRAWING

DRAWING

DRAWING

DRAWING

www.ingramcontent.com/pod-product-compliance
Lightning Source LLC
Chambersburg PA
CBHW060520130626
46553CB00002B/579